GRAPHIC ORGANIZERS FOR WRITING

IncentivePublications

*Written by Kathleen Bullock, Cherrie Farnette,
Marjorie Frank, and Jill Norris
Edited by Cary Grayson*

ISBN 978-0-86530-035-4

4   5   6   7   8   9   10   14   13   12   11

Printed by Sheridan Books, Inc., Chelsea, Michigan • November 2011
www.incentivepublications.com

Using Graphic Organizers

The use of graphic organizers as part of the writing process is important to writing success. Students who plan and write with graphic organizers:

- generate and organize more ideas,
- recall and analyze data,
- support main ideas with appropriate details,
- focus on the criteria for the specific writing assignment,
- explain sequences logically,
- recognize relationships between concepts,
- focus on their audience, and
- implement good writing techniques.

In his book, *Frames of Mind*, Howard Gardner discusses how the use of visuals engages a learner's multiple intelligences. The U.S. Department of Education reported that students with visible planning in writing scored higher on the National Assessment of Education Progress (NAEP) than those who did not plan.

Graphic Organizers for Writing is one resource every teacher needs. Here are 60 graphic organizers for writing nonfiction, fiction, and integrating explicit elements of good writing. Use the organizers to facilitate excellent writing.

Help your students organize for success!

Graphic Organizers

for

Nonfiction Writing

Writing an Essay

Step 1

Topic

Step 2

Introduction and Thesis Sentence

Step 3

Body

Example

Example

Example

● ● ●

● ● ●

● ● ●

Step 4

Conclusion

Step 5

Title

Name _____

I go buggy over your writing!

IP 925-2 • *Graphic Organizers for Writing*
©Incentive Publications, Inc., Nashville, TN.

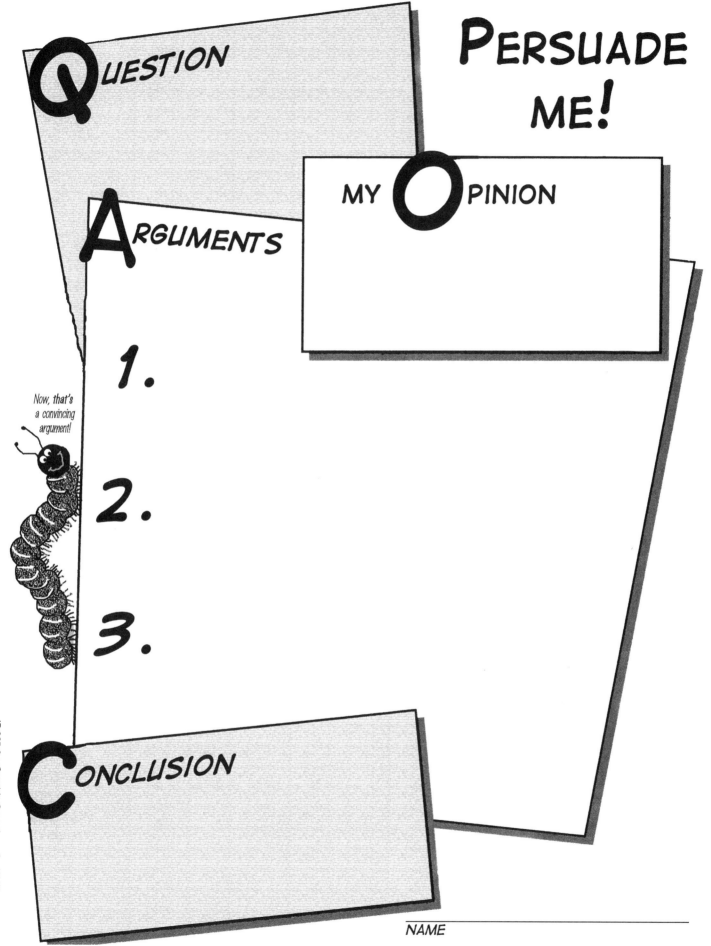

PERSUADE ME!

QUESTION

ARGUMENTS

MY **O**PINION

Now, that's a convincing argument!

1.

2.

3.

CONCLUSION

NAME

IP 925-2 • Graphic Organizers for Writing
©Incentive Publications, Inc., Nashville, TN.

GETTING STARTED

IDEAS ABOUT _____
                    TOPIC

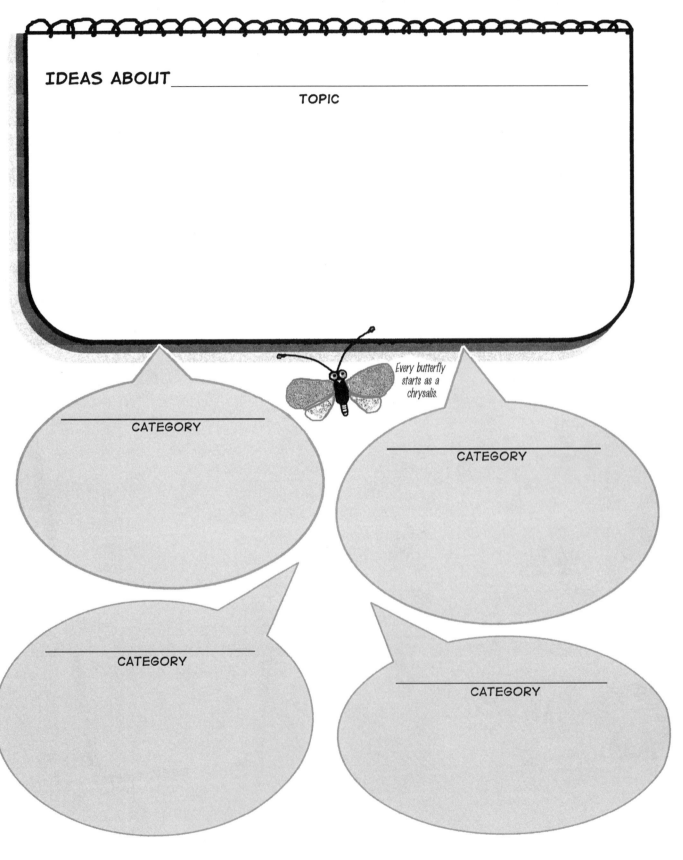

_____ CATEGORY

_____ CATEGORY

Every butterfly starts as a chrysalis.

_____ CATEGORY

_____ CATEGORY

NAME_____

IP 925-2 • Graphic Organizers for Writing
©Incentive Publications, Inc., Nashville, TN.

Report Organizer

Main Topic:

Subtopic:	Subtopic:	Subtopic:

- ●
- ●
- ●
- ●

Get smart, get organized.

Conclusion:

Name:_____

IP 925-2 • Graphic Organizers for Writing
©Incentive Publications, Inc., Nashville, TN.

Describe It!

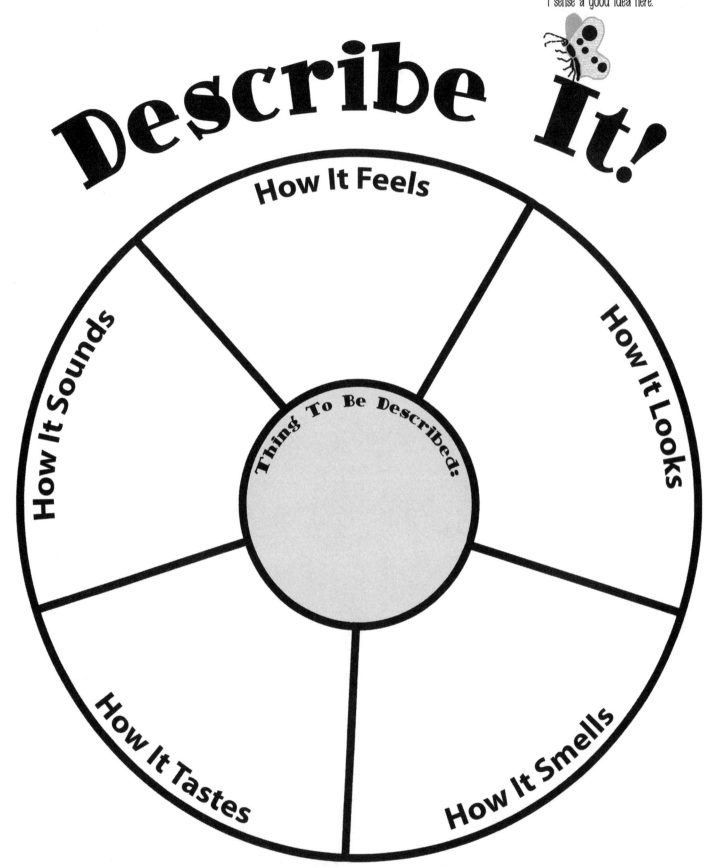

I sense a good idea here.

How It Feels

How It Looks

How It Sounds

How It Smells

How It Tastes

Thing To Be Described:

Name:_____

IP 925-2 • *Graphic Organizers for Writing*
©Incentive Publications, Inc., Nashville, TN.

Writing How-To

Job

Materials

HOW TO KNIT 100 SOCKS IN 24 HOURS
BY MILLIE PEDE

Writing down the steps was very helpful.

Step by Step_____

1.

2.

3.

4

5.

Name:_____

IP 925-2 • *Graphic Organizers for Writing*
©Incentive Publications, Inc., Nashville, TN.

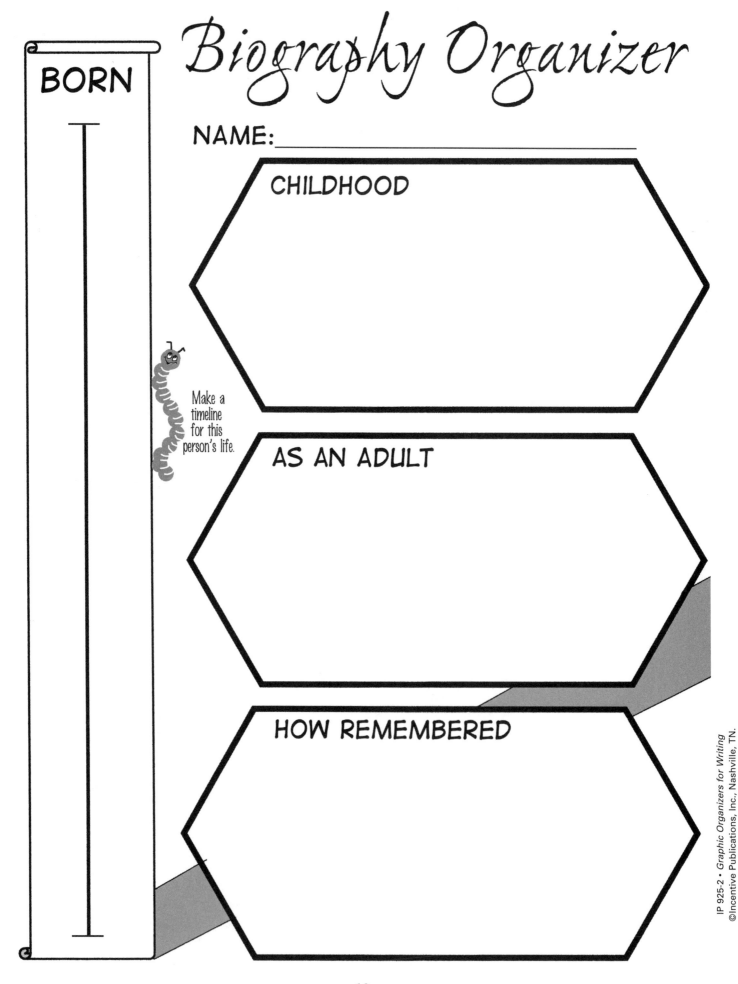

Biography Organizer

BORN

NAME:_____

CHILDHOOD

AS AN ADULT

HOW REMEMBERED

Make a timeline for this person's life.

10

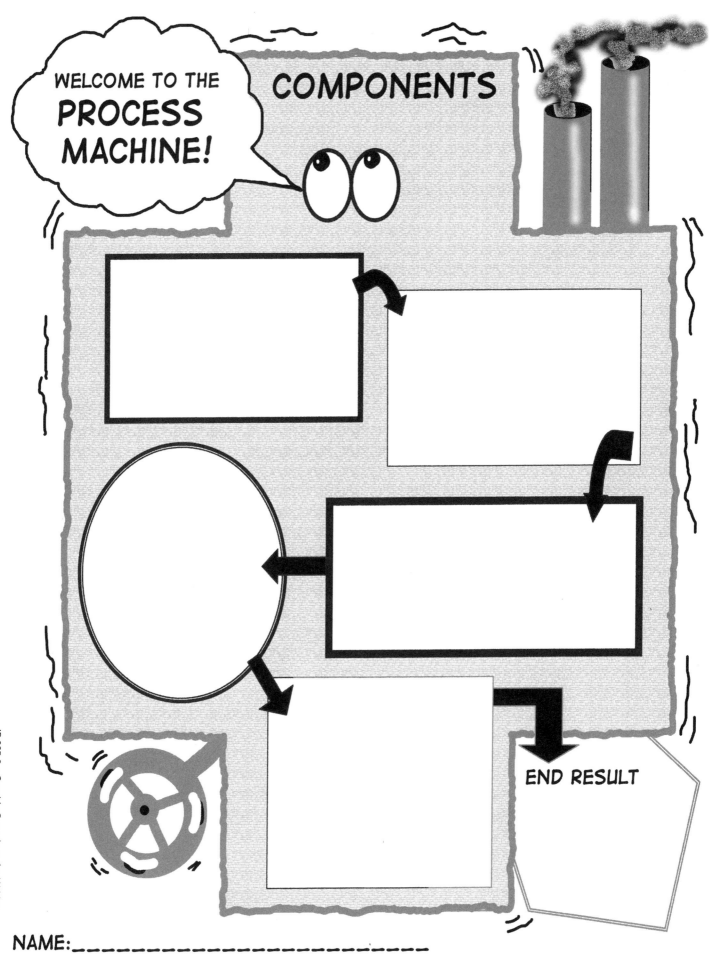

IP 925-2 • Graphic Organizers for Writing
©Incentive Publications, Inc., Nashville, TN.

NAME:_____

Chain of Events

Starting Point

Name:_____

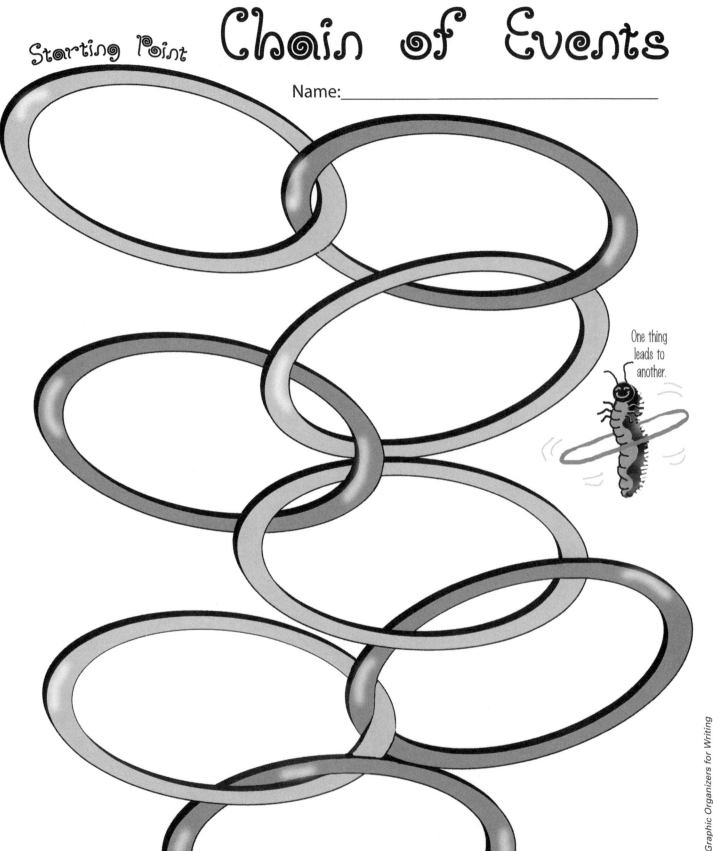

One thing leads to another.

End Result

IP 925-2 • *Graphic Organizers for Writing*
©Incentive Publications, Inc., Nashville, TN.

IT'S A CYCLE!

NAME OF THE CYCLE

I go in circles when I cycle.

Name:_____

IP 925-2 • *Graphic Organizers for Writing*
© Incentive Publications, Inc., Nashville, TN.

Autobiography
Rocket

Name:_____

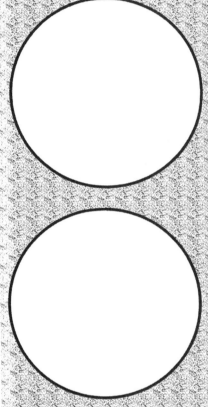
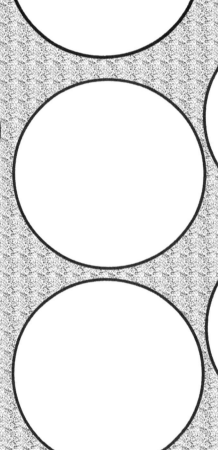

Me

1. Write your name or draw your picture.
2. Fill some circles with an important person, place, or event.
3. List your special talents in the remaining circles.

IP 925-2 • *Graphic Organizers for Writing*
©Incentive Publications, Inc., Nashville, TN.

BARE-BONES REPORTING

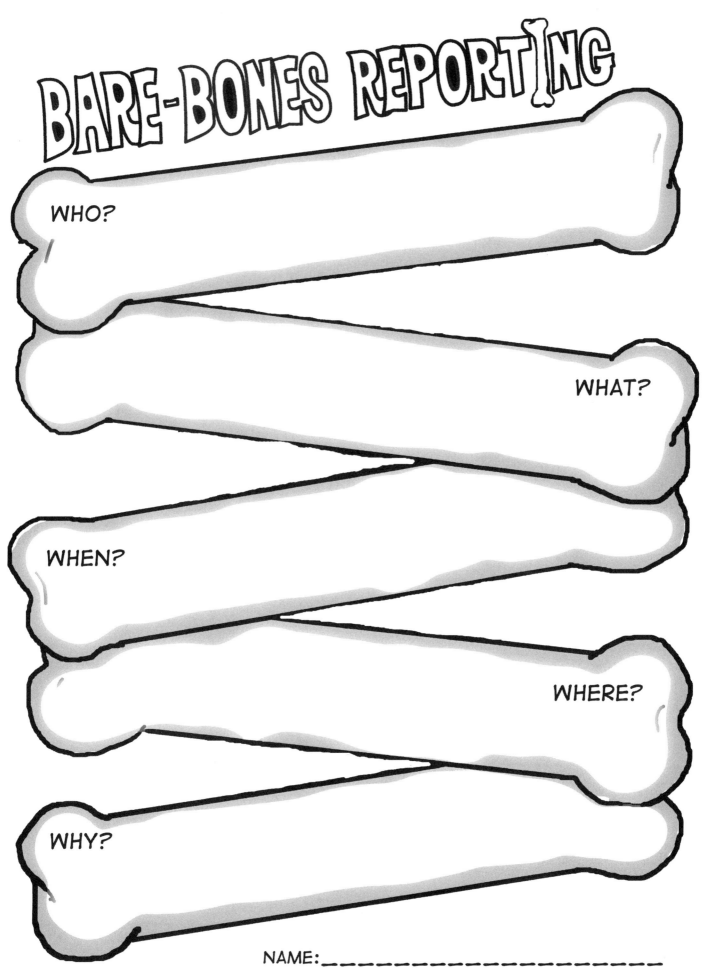

WHO?

WHAT?

WHEN?

WHERE?

WHY?

NAME:_____

IP 925-2 • Graphic Organizers for Writing
©Incentive Publications, Inc., Nashville, TN.

Problem – Solution

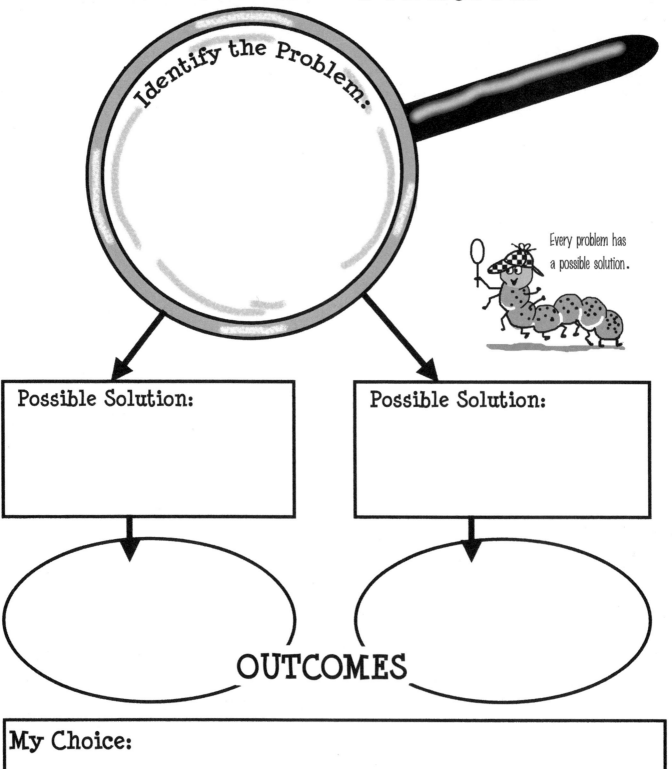

Identify the Problem:

Every problem has a possible solution.

Possible Solution:

Possible Solution:

OUTCOMES

My Choice:

Name:_____

IP 925-2 • *Graphic Organizers for Writing*
©Incentive Publications, Inc., Nashville, TN.

Personal Narrative

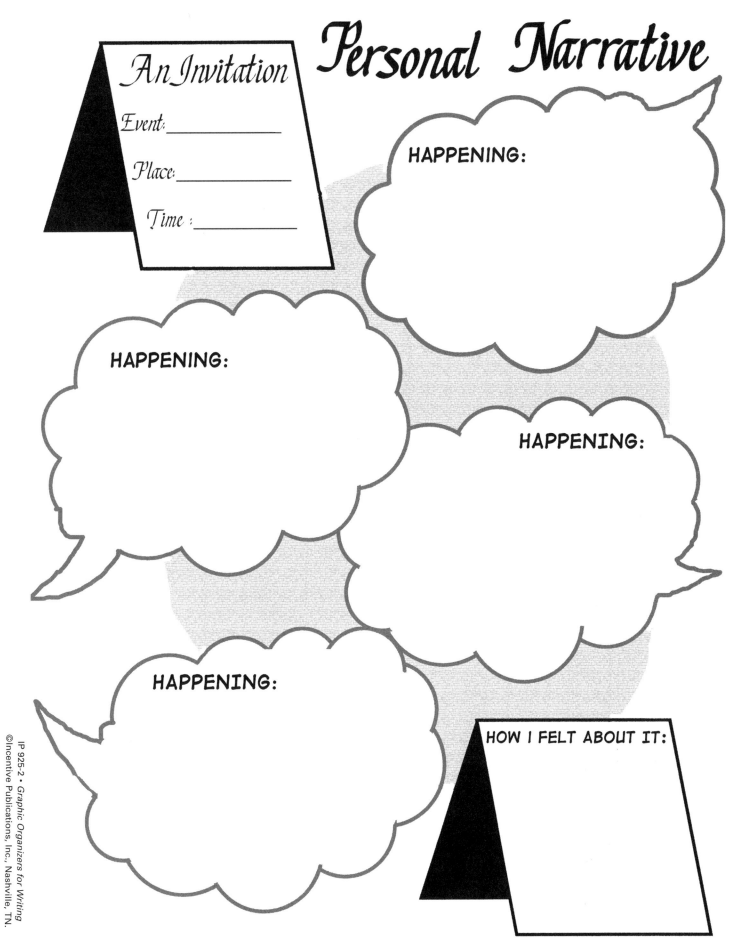

An Invitation

Event: _____

Place: _____

Time : _____

HAPPENING:

HAPPENING:

HAPPENING:

HAPPENING:

HOW I FELT ABOUT IT:

IP 925-2 • *Graphic Organizers for Writing*
©Incentive Publications, Inc., Nashville, TN.

NAME: _____

Newsworthy Reporting

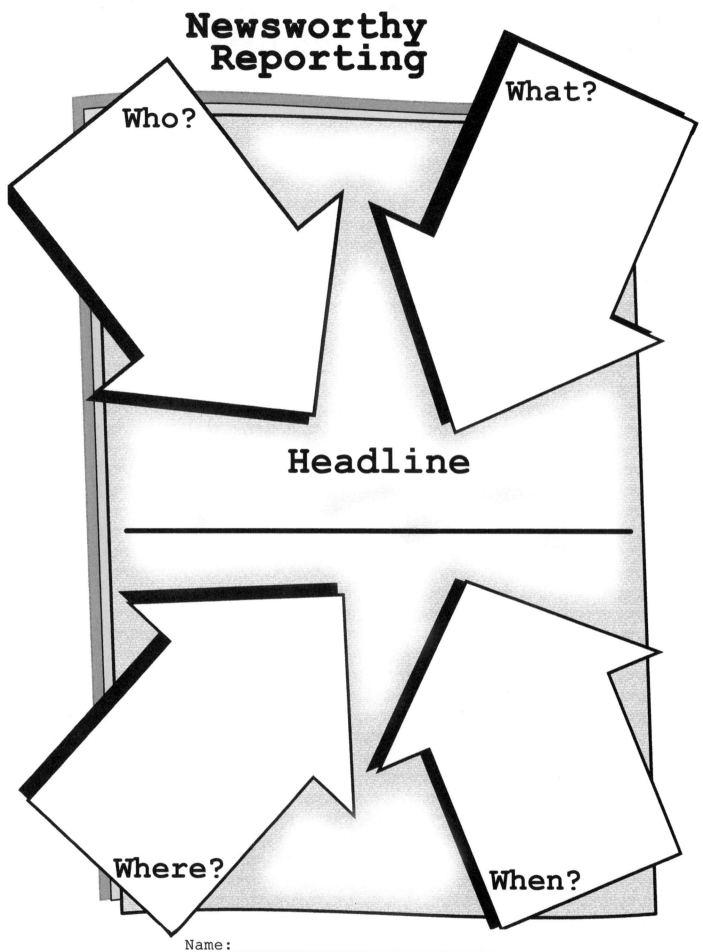

Who?

What?

Headline

_____

Where?

When?

Name:_____

IP 925-2 • *Graphic Organizers for Writing*
©Incentive Publications, Inc., Nashville, TN.

Writing a News Article

1 Get the facts: Who?

When?   How?

What?   Where?

2 Write an opening sentence.

3 Write the body of the article.

4 Create a headline.

Name: _____

IP 925-2 • Graphic Organizers for Writing
©Incentive Publications, Inc., Nashville, TN.

INTERVIEW

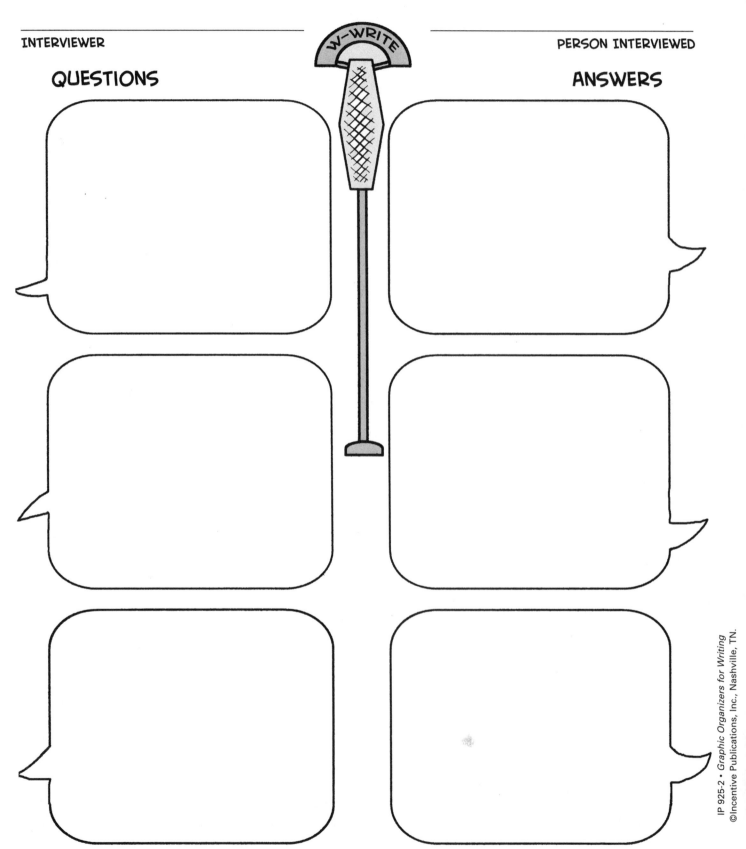

INTERVIEWER _____

QUESTIONS

PERSON INTERVIEWED

ANSWERS

W-WRITE

IP 925-2 • Graphic Organizers for Writing
©Incentive Publications, Inc., Nashville, TN.

A Friendly Letter

Date

Greeting

,

Body

Closing

,

Signature

IP 925-2 • Graphic Organizers for Writing
©Incentive Publications, Inc., Nashville, TN.

Name:_____

A Formal Letter

Return Address

Date

Inside Address

Greeting

:

Body

Closing

,

Signature

Name:_____

IP 925-2 • *Graphic Organizers for Writing*
©Incentive Publications, Inc., Nashville, TN.

An Invitation

Occasion

Why

When

Host

Where

How to Respond

IP 925-2 • *Graphic Organizers for Writing*
©Incentive Publications, Inc., Nashville, TN.

KEYS TO SUCCESS

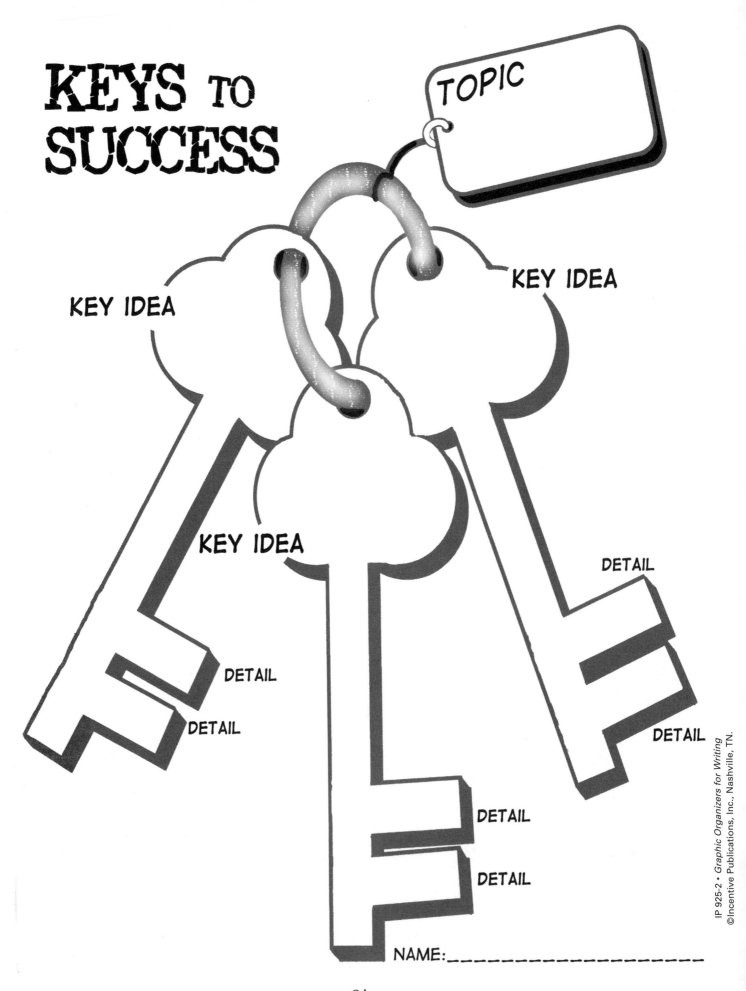

TOPIC

KEY IDEA

KEY IDEA

KEY IDEA

DETAIL

DETAIL

DETAIL

DETAIL

DETAIL

DETAIL

NAME:_____

24

IP 925-2 • *Graphic Organizers for Writing*
©Incentive Publications, Inc., Nashville, TN.

Comparing Two Times

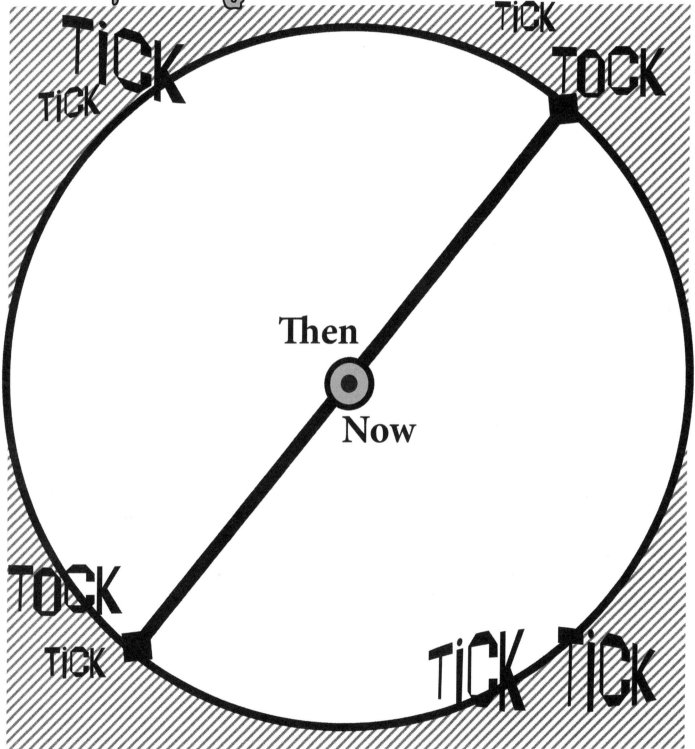

IP 925-2 • *Graphic Organizers for Writing*
©Incentive Publications, Inc., Nashville, TN.

Name:_____

GATHERING INFORMATION

Notes

Source:

Author:

Publisher:

Date of Publication:

Page:

Notes

Notes

Source:

Author:

Publisher:

Date of Publication:

Page:

Notes

Source:

Author:

Publisher:

Date of Publication:

Page:

Name:

IP 925-2 • Graphic Organizers for Writing
©Incentive Publications, Inc., Nashville, TN.

Wedding Cake Summary

In summary, this cake looks good enough to eat.

TOPIC:_____

SYNONYM FOR TOPIC:

_____

NEWS HEADLINE EXPRESSING A MAJOR IDEA RELATED TO TOPIC:

_____

THREE ATTRIBUTES DESCRIBING THE TOPIC:

INSIGHT GAINED FROM STUDYING THE TOPIC:

HOW MIGHT THIS TOPIC CHANGE IN THE NEXT 25 YEARS?

NAME:_____

IP 925-2 • *Graphic Organizers for Writing*
©Incentive Publications, Inc., Nashville, TN.

Idea Web

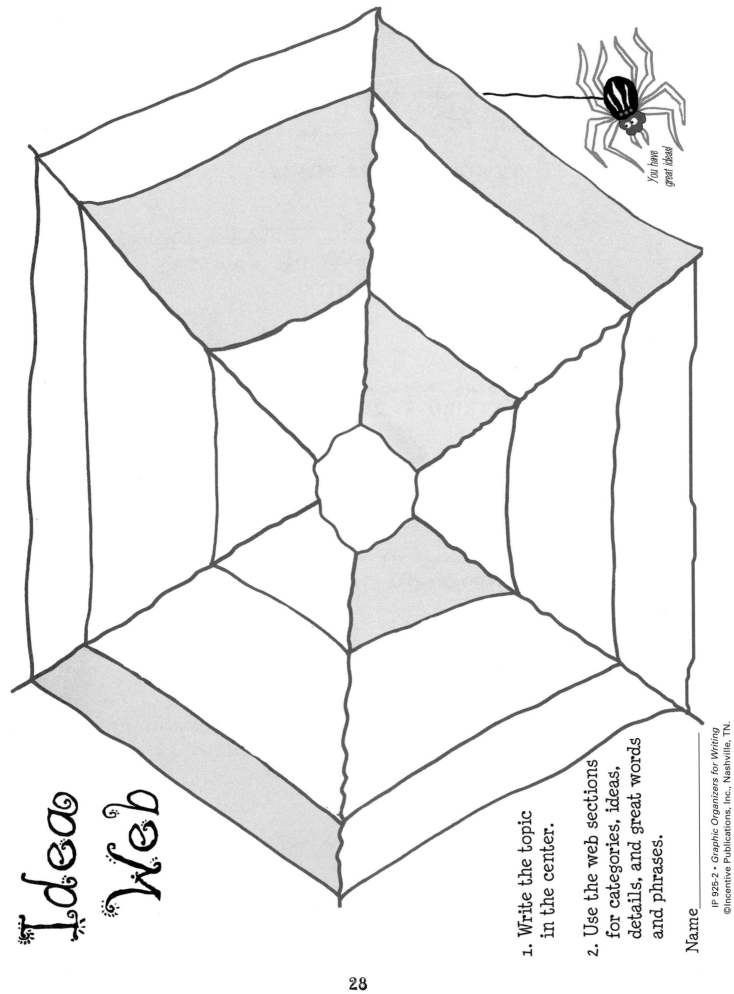

You have great ideas!

1. Write the topic in the center.

2. Use the web sections for categories, ideas, details, and great words and phrases.

Name _____

IP 925-2 • *Graphic Organizers for Writing*
©Incentive Publications, Inc., Nashville, TN.

Graphic Organizers
for
Fiction Writing

Tinker With It! Building a Story

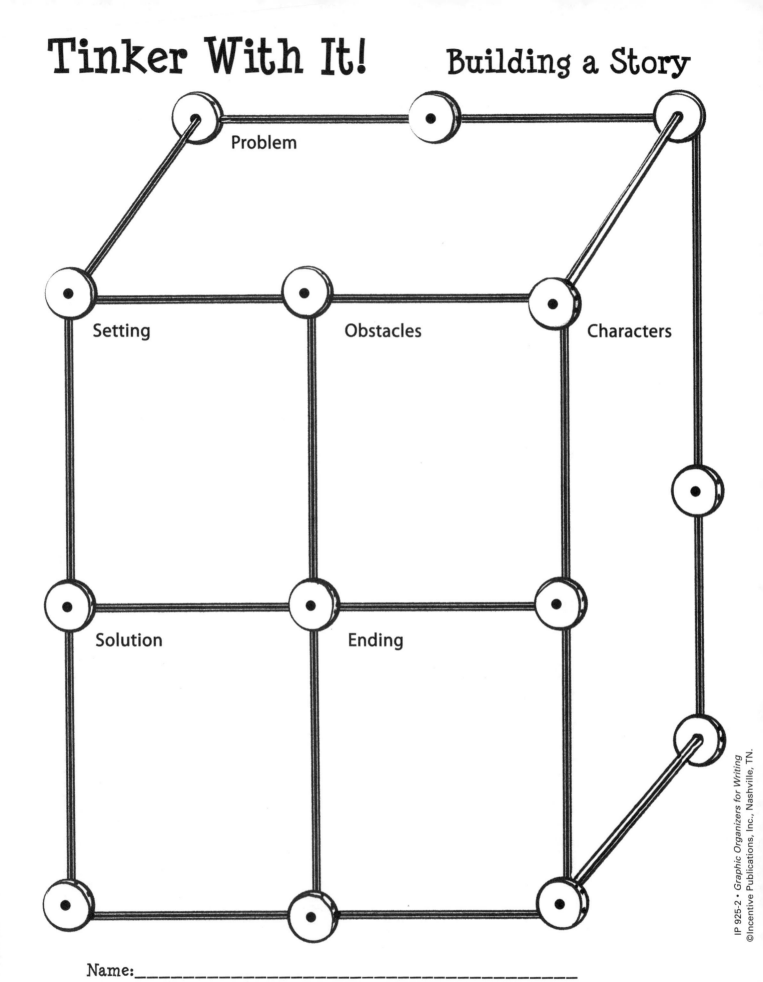

Problem

Setting   Obstacles   Characters

Solution   Ending

Name:_____

IP 925-2 • *Graphic Organizers for Writing*
©Incentive Publications, Inc., Nashville, TN.

Planning A Story Setting

Place

Specific Place:

Descriptive Words and Phrases:

Time

Specific Time:

Characteristics of the Time:

IP 925-2 • Graphic Organizers for Writing
©Incentive Publications, Inc., Nashville, TN.

Name:_____

Description Highlights

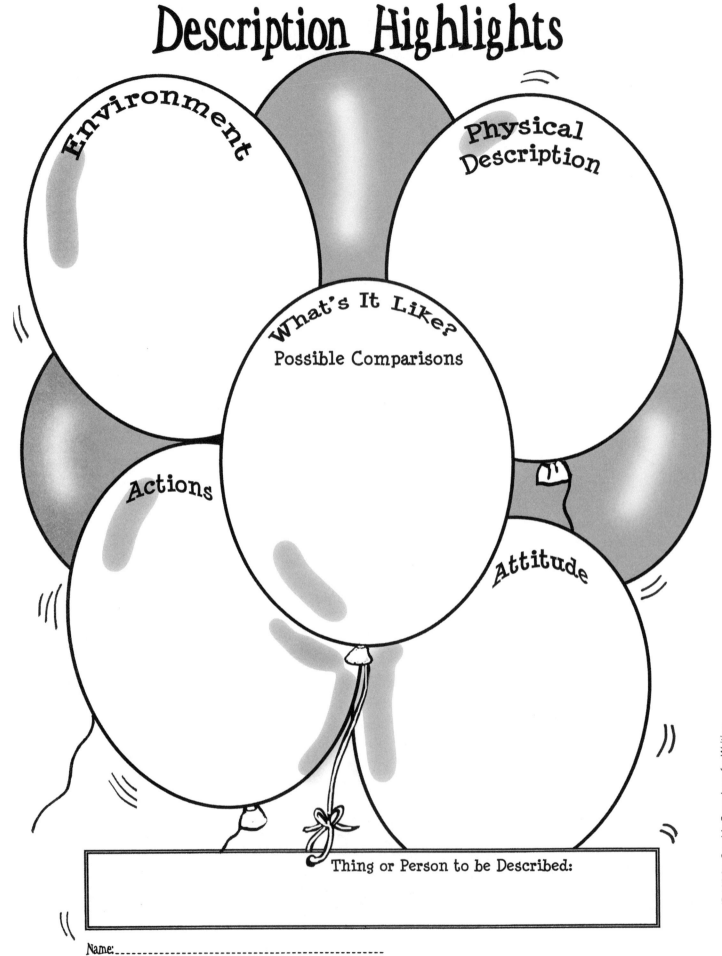

Environment

Physical Description

What's It Like?

Possible Comparisons

Actions

Attitude

Thing or Person to be Described:

Name:

IP 925-2 • *Graphic Organizers for Writing*
©Incentive Publications, Inc., Nashville, TN.

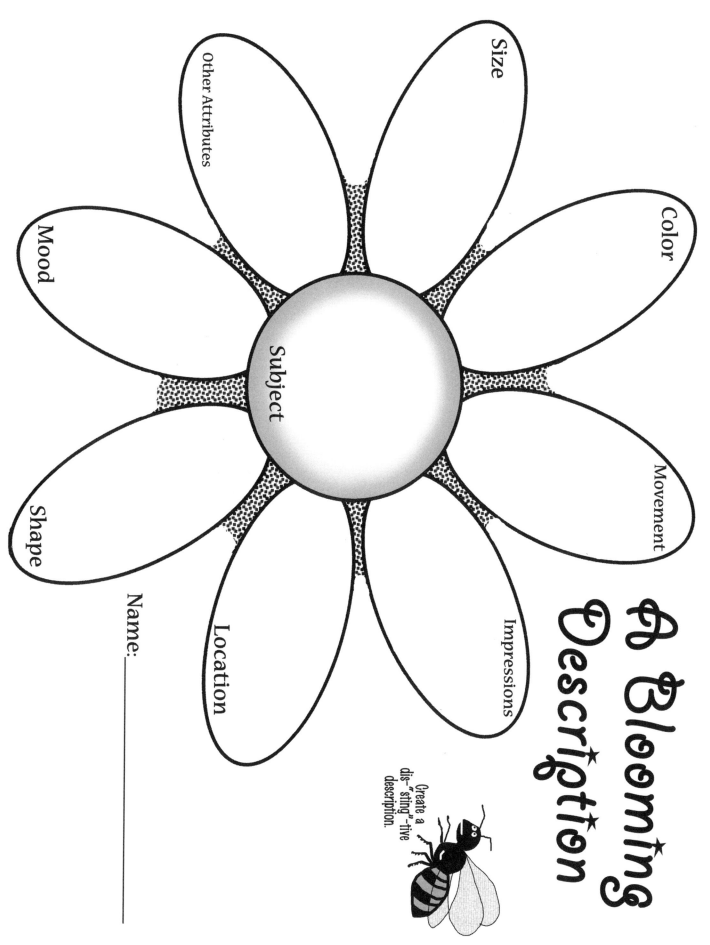

A Blooming Description

Create a dis-"sting"-tive description.

Subject

Size

Color

Movement

Impressions

Location

Shape

Mood

Other Attributes

Name: _____

IP 925-2 • Graphic Organizers for Writing
©Incentive Publications, Inc., Nashville, TN.

Plan the "Print" Your Character Will Leave

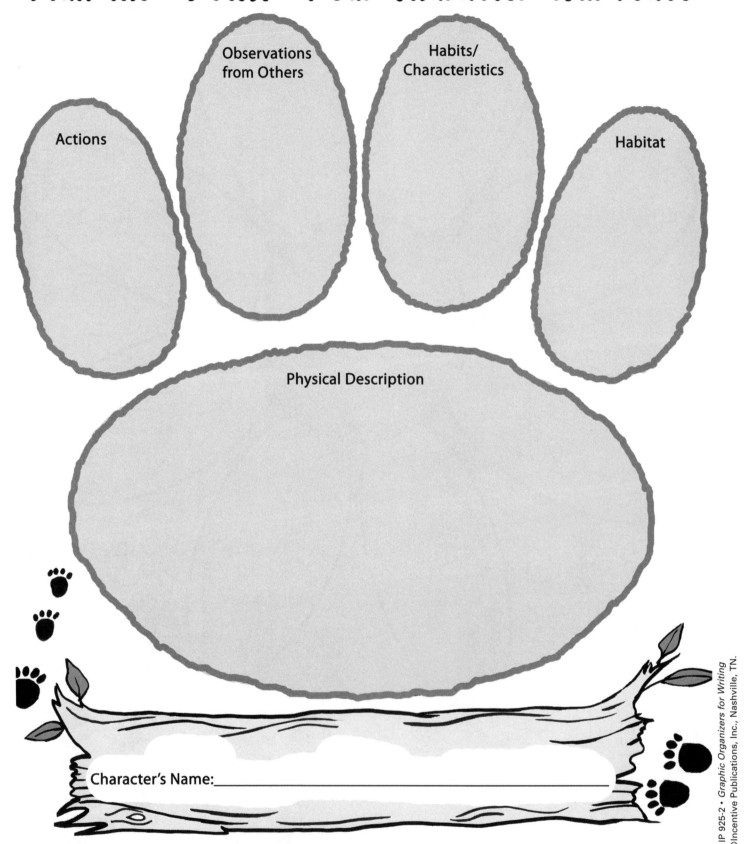

Actions

Observations from Others

Habits/ Characteristics

Habitat

Physical Description

Character's Name:_____

Name:_____

IP 925-2 • *Graphic Organizers for Writing*
©Incentive Publications, Inc., Nashville, TN.

Cause & Effect

SITUATION ONE

CAUSE

EFFECT

What caused these spots?

SITUATION TWO

CAUSE

EFFECT

IP 925-2 • Graphic Organizers for Writing
©Incentive Publications, Inc., Nashville, TN.

Name:_____

Add a Twist

Twist

Events

Conclusion

Events

In the Beginning

Setting

Events

Characters

_____'s Story Planner

36

IP 925-2 • *Graphic Organizers for Writing*
©Incentive Publications, Inc., Nashville, TN.

Stringing a Variety of Sentences

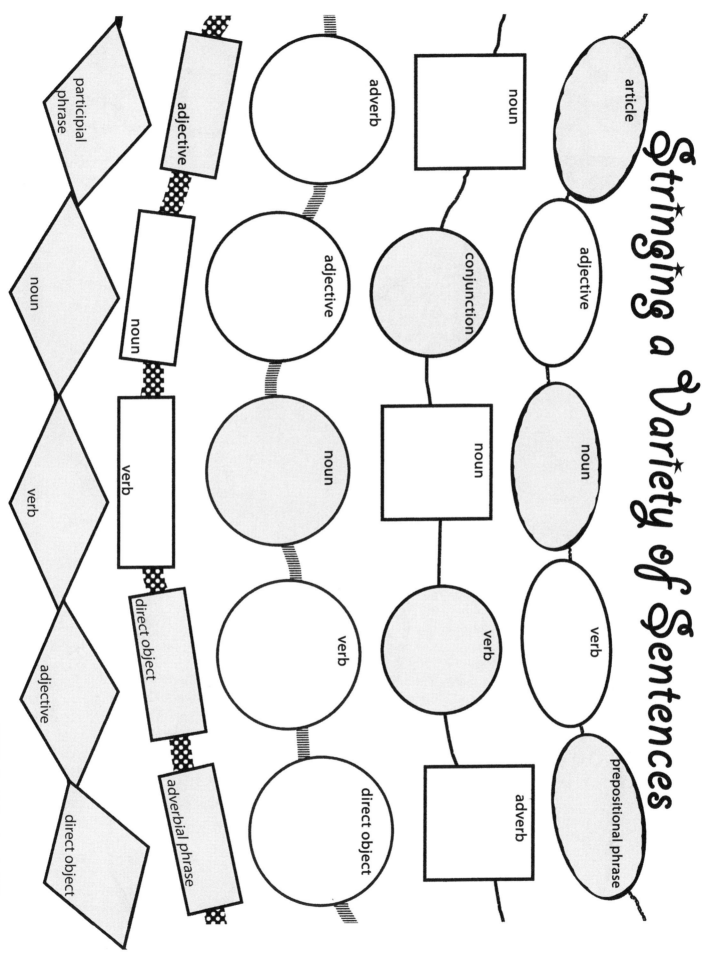

article

adjective

noun

conjunction

adjective

noun

verb

prepositional phrase

verb

adverb

direct object

noun

verb

adjective

noun

verb

adverb

noun

direct object

participial phrase

noun

verb

adjective

direct object

adjective

noun

verb

direct object

adverbial phrase

IP 925-2 • *Graphic Organizers for Writing*
©Incentive Publications, Inc., Nashville, TN.

Spice it Up!

Topic _____

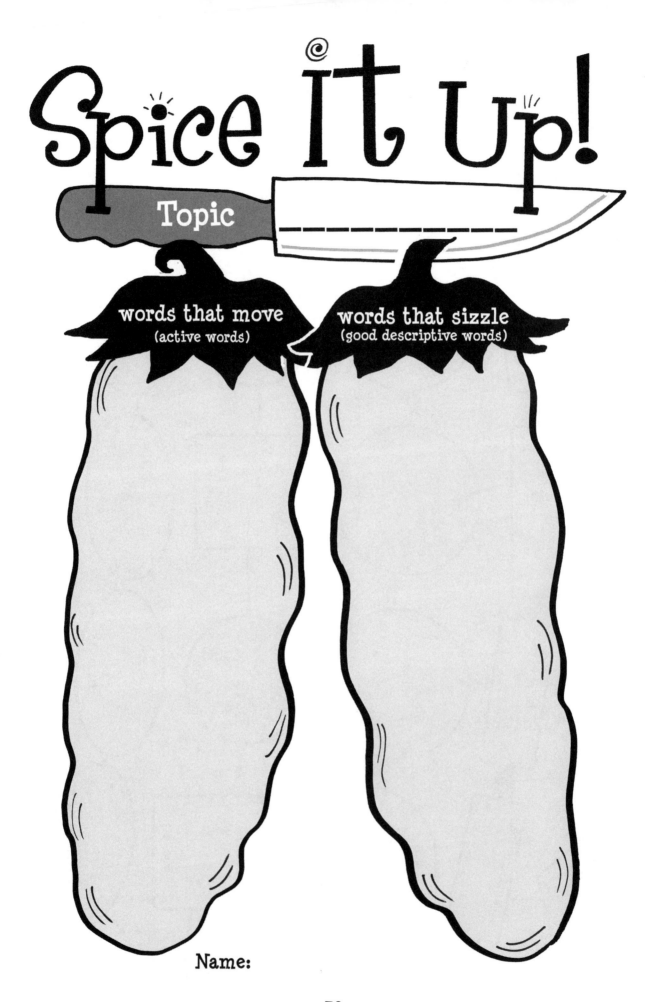

words that move
(active words)

words that sizzle
(good descriptive words)

Name:

IP 925-2 • Graphic Organizers for Writing
©Incentive Publications, Inc., Nashville, TN.

Name:_____

WRITE AN ALTERNATE
ENDING

EXISTING ENDING

WHAT WILL I CHANGE?

HOW WILL IT AFFECT THE STORY?

DESCRIPTION OF NEW ENDING

MESSAGE IN A RAINBOW

IMPORTANT IDEAS

COLORFUL WORDS

SYMBOLISM

COMPARISONS

Good writing is worth a pot of gold.

NAME:_____

IP 925-2 • *Graphic Organizers for Writing*
©Incentive Publications, Inc., Nashville, TN.

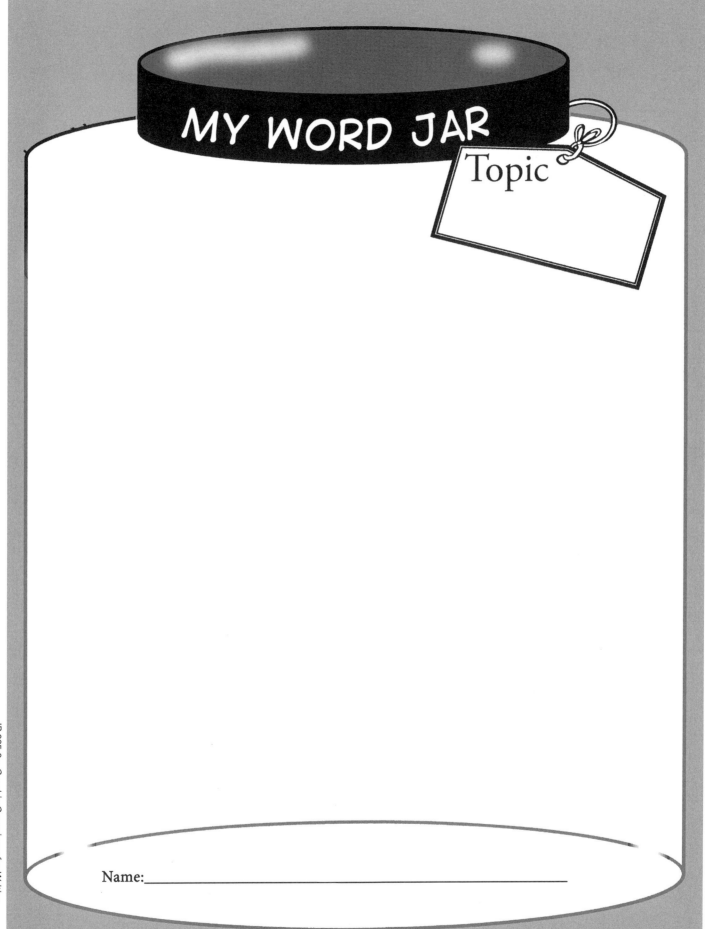

MY WORD JAR

Topic

Name:_____

IP 925-2 • *Graphic Organizers for Writing*
©Incentive Publications, Inc., Nashville, TN.

Create a Simple Rhyme

Rhyming Word Pairs

Try using these rhyming patterns, and create one of your own..

aabb   abac   abcb

abcc   aaa   abb

_____

IP 925-2 • *Graphic Organizers for Writing*
©Incentive Publications, Inc., Nashville, TN.

Name:_____

Decision Organizer for Writing Poetry

TOPIC:

Type of Poem:

- *couplet*
- free verse
- **definition**
- haiku
- limerick
- _____

Rhyming: ___yes ___no

Word Bank

IP 925-2 • *Graphic Organizers for Writing*
©Incentive Publications, Inc., Nashville, TN.

Name:_____

Writing a Fairytale

Setting

Characters
(Label them good
or evil)

Magic

Problem
& Solution

- [ ] Special Beginnings (Once upon a time...)
- [ ] Special Endings (...and they lived happily ever after.)
- [ ] Problem & Solution
- [ ] Things in Threes or Sevens
- [ ] Good & Evil Characters
- [ ] Royalty and/or Castle
- [ ] Magic

Name:_____

IP 925-2 • Graphic Organizers for Writing
©Incentive Publications, Inc., Nashville, TN.

Writing a Fable

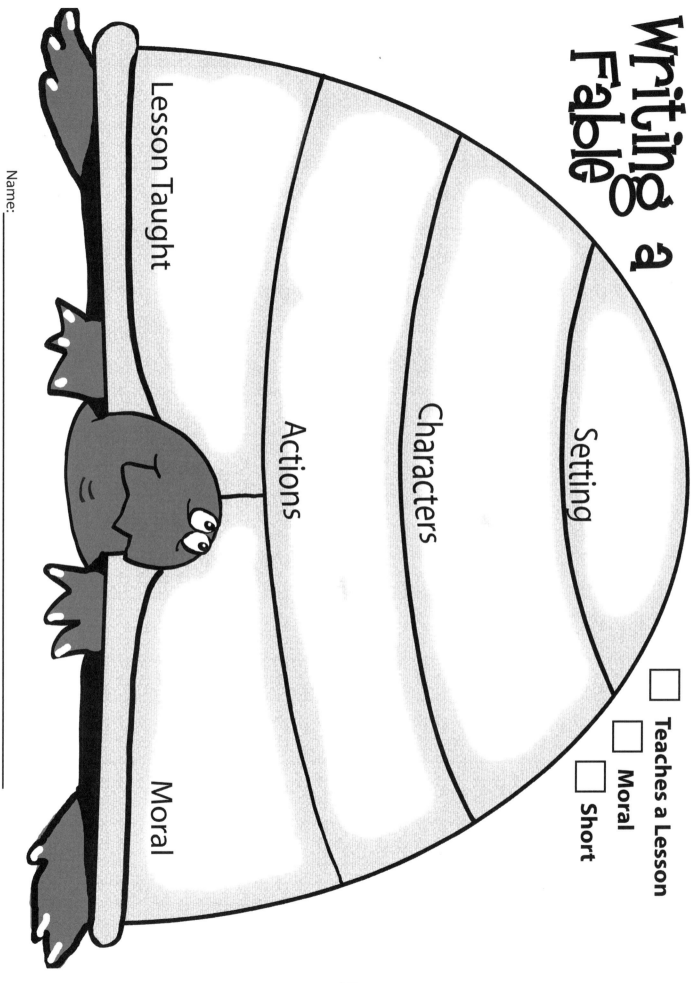

Lesson Taught

Actions

Characters

Setting

Moral

- [ ] Teaches a Lesson
- [ ] Moral
- [ ] Short

Name: _____

IP 925-2 • *Graphic Organizers for Writing*
©Incentive Publications, Inc., Nashville, TN.

Writing A Mystery

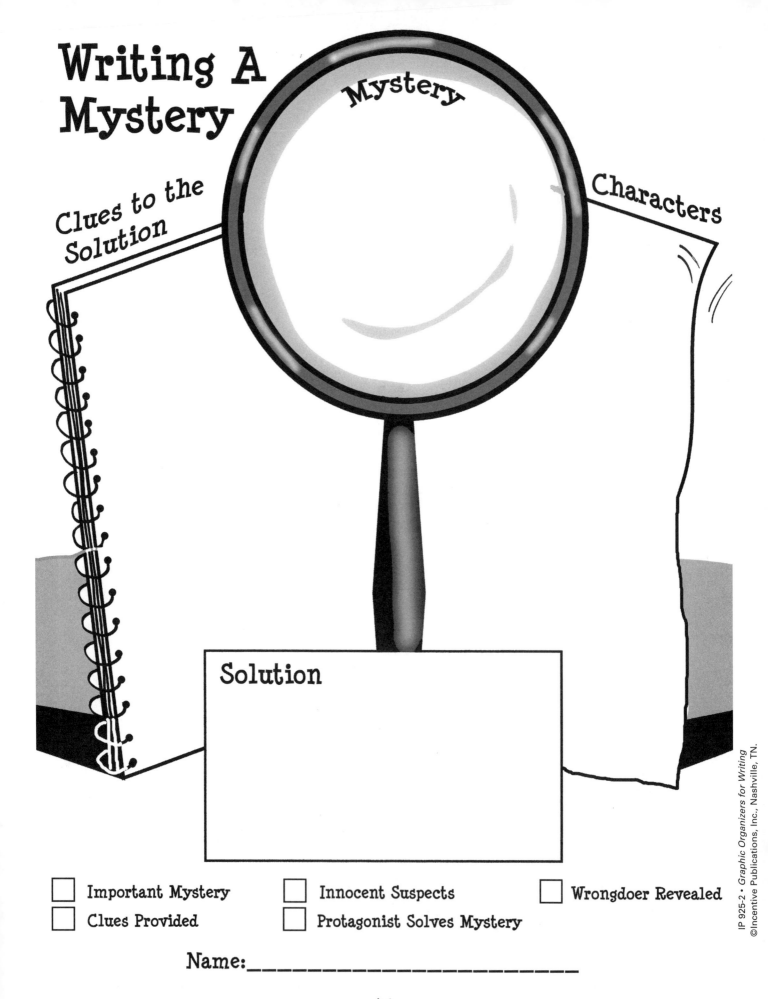

Mystery

Clues to the Solution

Characters

Solution

☐ Important Mystery   ☐ Innocent Suspects   ☐ Wrongdoer Revealed

☐ Clues Provided   ☐ Protagonist Solves Mystery

Name:_____

IP 925-2 • Graphic Organizers for Writing
©Incentive Publications, Inc., Nashville, TN.

Graphic Organizers

for

Teacher Organizers

Good Beginnings

Attention-Grabbing Beginnings

A good beginning catches the reader's attention. It gives a hint about what is going to happen or what is going to be argued. Yet, it doesn't give away the whole story, explanation, or argument. A good beginning makes the reader curious enough to continue.

Draft of Beginning:

Checklist

- ☐ grabs the reader's attention
- ☐ states the main idea or topic
- ☐ sets the stage
- ☐ makes a surprising statement
- ☐ states unusual facts
- ☐ uses fascinating quotes
- ☐ poses questions to be asked
- ☐ includes quips about famous character
- ☐ contains strong opinions

Revised Beginning:

Name:_____

IP 925-2 • *Graphic Organizers for Writing*
©Incentive Publications, Inc., Nashville, TN.

Good Endings

A strong ending is as important as a good beginning. Like the opening, your conclusion will depend on the topic, form, and purpose of the writing. Yet for each piece of writing, there are many possible ways to wrap it up. That's what your ending must do. It must drive the point home, solidify your argument, or tie up the tale with gusto.

Points To Be Included:

Draft of Ending:

Revised Ending:

Checklist

- ☐ restates or reviews thesis
- ☐ summarizes the meaning of the composition
- ☐ leaves the main point firmly in the reader's mind
- ☐ keeps the reader's attention right to the end
- ☐ gives a final wrap-up quote
- ☐ poses questions for the reader
- ☐ provides a lesson or moral
- ☐ relates a surprising turn of events or unexpected solution
- ☐ creates a mystery that leaves the reader wondering

Name:_____

IP 925-2 • *Graphic Organizers for Writing*
©Incentive Publications, Inc., Nashville, TN.

Figurative Language Checklist

Name:_____

☐ **Metaphor** - comparison of two unlike things
Our dog is a vacuum cleaner lapping up every crumb.

Example from my writing:

☐ **Simile** - comparison of two unlike things using *as* or *like*
My computer is like a grammar coach looking over my shoulder.

Example from my writing:

My web is like a magnet.

☐ **Alliteration** - repetition of consonant sounds at the beginning of words
flimsy flippers flailing and flopping

Example from my writing:

☐ **Onomatopoeia** - use of words that sound like the thing they name
Bang! Hiss! Pop! Splat!

Example from my writing:

Buzzzzz

☐ **Personification** - a nonliving thing is given human characteristics
The pop-up screen grabbed me and dragged me onto the website.

Example from my writing:

IP 925-2 • *Graphic Organizers for Writing*
©Incentive Publications, Inc., Nashville, TN.

Editing Checklist

Content
___Is the introduction interesting?
___Does the introduction contain an identifiable thesis statement?
___Is the body of the writing logically organized?
___Does the information presented stick to the topic?
___Are all ideas and paragraphs well developed and clearly explained?
___Does the conclusion summarize and clarify important information?

Style
___Are all paragraphs well developed?
___Do paragraphs begin in a variety of ways?
___Does each paragraph have a topic sentence?
___Are the words carefully chosen for meaning and explicit description?
___Is the writing grammatically correct?
___Is the writing punctuated correctly?
___Are all words spelled correctly?

Format
___Does the writing have correct margins, spacing, and headings?
___Are all paragraphs indented properly?

Name:_____

IP 925-2 • Graphic Organizers for Writing
©Incentive Publications, Inc., Nashville, TN.

Name:_____

Content
___Is the introduction interesting?
___Does the introduction contain an identifiable thesis statement?
___Is the body of the writing logically organized?
___Does the information presented stick to the topic?
___Are all ideas and paragraphs well developed and clearly explained?
___Does the conclusion summarize and clarify important information?

Style
___Are all paragraphs well developed?
___Do paragraphs begin in a variety of ways?
___Does each paragraph have a topic sentence?
___Are the words carefully chosen for meaning and explicit description?
___Is the writing grammatically correct?
___Is the writing punctuated correctly?
___Are all words spelled correctly?

Format
___Does the writing have correct margins, spacing, and headings?
___Are all paragraphs indented properly?

Editing Checklist

Name:_____

Writing Response Plan

Point out and praise successes.

Ask questions that will help the author review and think about writing.

The author puts *praise* and *questions* to good use to complete the composition.

IP 925-2 • *Graphic Organizers for Writing*
©Incentive Publications, Inc., Nashville, TN.

Writing Record

Name: _____

Class _____

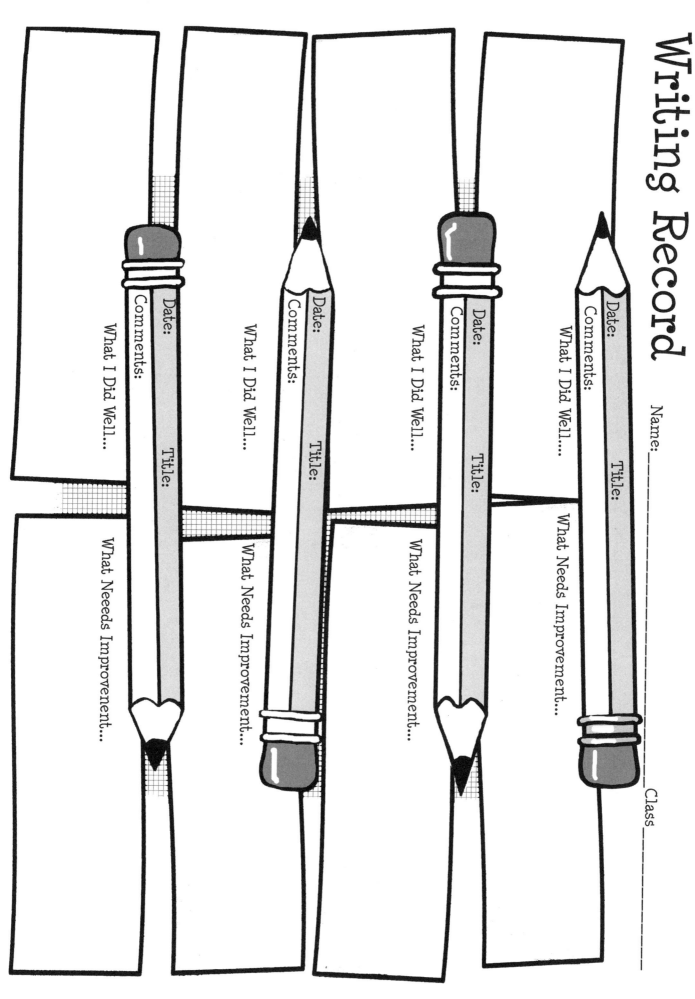

Date:

Comments:

Title:

What I Did Well...

What Needs Improvement...

Date:

Comments:

Title:

What I Did Well...

What Needs Improvement...

Date:

Comments:

Title:

What I Did Well...

What Needs Improvement...

Date:

Comments:

Title:

What I Did Well...

What Needs Improvement...

IP 925-2 • *Graphic Organizers for Writing*
©Incentive Publications, Inc., Nashville, TN.

WRITING RUBRIC Name: _____

Elements to be Evaluated	Beginning Writer	Developing Writer	Accomplished Writer	Advanced Writer
	Description of Element at this Level	Description of Element at this Level	Description of Element at this Level	Description of Element at this Level

IP 925-2 • Graphic Organizers for Writing
©Incentive Publications, Inc., Nashville, TN.

IP 925-2 • *Graphic Organizers for Writing*
©Incentive Publications, Inc., Nashville, TN.

IP 925-2 • *Graphic Organizers for Writing*
©Incentive Publications, Inc., Nashville, TN.

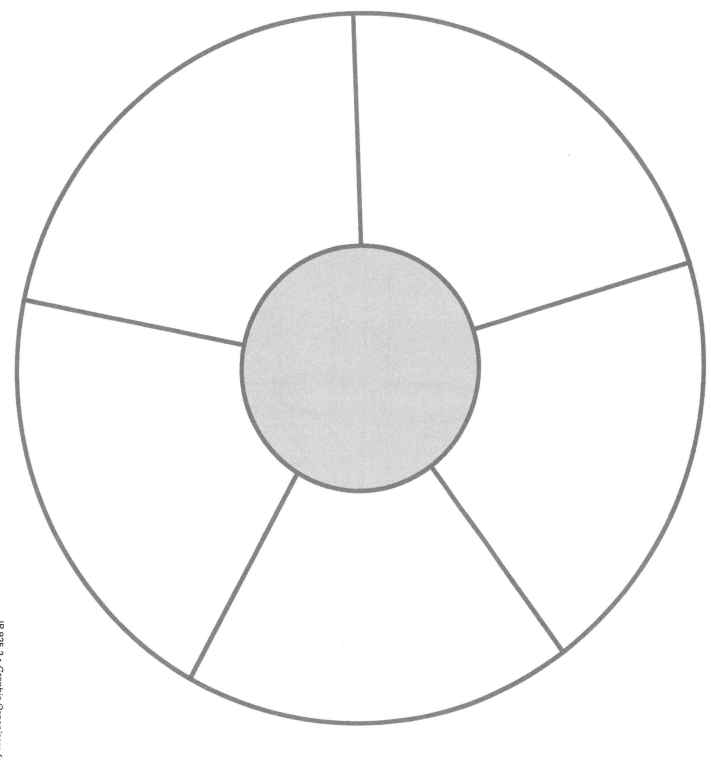

IP 925-2 • *Graphic Organizers for Writing*
©Incentive Publications, Inc., Nashville, TN.

IP 925-2 • *Graphic Organizers for Writing*
©Incentive Publications, Inc., Nashville, TN.

IP 925-2 • *Graphic Organizers for Writing*
©Incentive Publications, Inc., Nashville, TN.

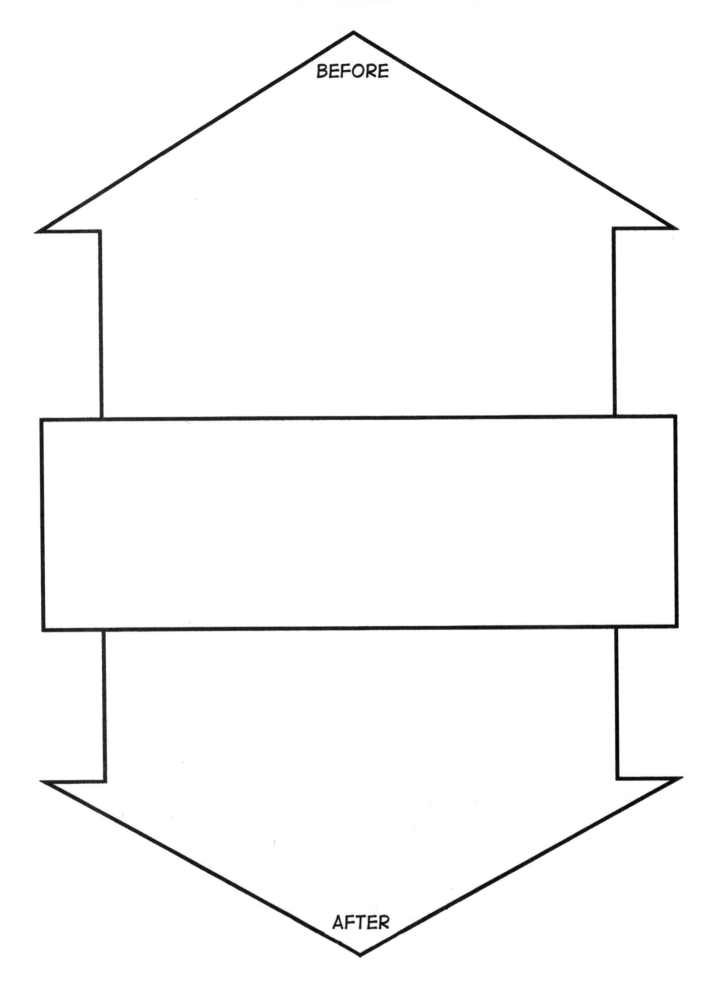

BEFORE

AFTER

IP 925-2 • *Graphic Organizers for Writing*
©Incentive Publications, Inc., Nashville, TN.

CHARACTER OR EVENT

VIEWPOINT 1   VIEWPOINT 2   VIEWPOINT 3

IP 925-2 • *Graphic Organizers for Writing*
©Incentive Publications, Inc., Nashville, TN.